301
FIRST GRADE
Questions & Answers

Illustrated by Michele Ackerman, Marie Allen, Martha Avilés, Tiphanie Beeke, Michelle Berg, Sharon Cartwright, David Austin Clar, Kevin L. Cuasay, Louise Gardner, Kallen Godsey, Thea Kliros, Kate Kolososki, Lindsey McCool, Michael Miller, Margie Moore, Robin Moro, Chris Moroney, Nicholas Myers, Burgandy Nilles, Ryan Sias, Susan Spellman, Nicole Tadgell, Peggy Tagel, Jeremy Tugeau, George Ulrich, Ted Williams, David Wojtowycz, and Maria Woods

Photography © DigitalVision, PhotoDisc, Brand X, iStock, Shutterstock, Media Bakery, Jupiter Images Unlimited, Art Explosion, ImageClub, Siede Preis Photography, and Brian Warling Photography

Published by Sequoia Children's Publishing, a division of Phoenix International Publications, Inc.

8501 West Higgins Road
Chicago, Illinois 60631

59 Gloucester Place
London W1U 8JJ

www.sequoiakidsbooks.com

ISBN 978-1-64269-331-7

Welcome to Active Minds!

Get ready for an exciting kind of early-learning activity! These 301 questions tackle key benchmarks across core categories such as language arts and math, as well as science, social sciences, physical and emotional development, fine arts, and foreign language. Categories are scattered throughout the book, and questions progress from easy to hard for a graduated learning experience. Colorful illustrations and photography help to present the material in a fun and engaging way. Answer keys for all questions are located in the last section of the book. Settle down, open the book, and have fun learning with your child today.

How to Use

- Open to the desired set of questions.

- Read the questions aloud. Ask your child to point to or name the answer.

- Answer keys are at the back of the book

Some Tips

- Your child might not be familiar with all of the content on these pages. Take the time to introduce new concepts and characters when these kinds of questions come up.

- Encourage your child to use the book with friends and/or siblings, too. Take turns asking each other the questions. The material might serve as a good review for older children!

- Be positive and encouraging. Learning should be fun! When your child seems tired, frustrated, or unfocused, take a break. You can always play again later.

Which word has the same ending sound as nest?

East   **South**

Which two groups have an equal number of fruits?

Which animal starts the same way as goose?

Is the girl doing gymnastics or gymnasium?

Questions

Fill in the missing note to finish the pattern.

You have five ice pops. Your friend has two. How many ice pops do you have together?

You have two quarters. Point to what you can buy.

50¢   25¢   95¢

Which word has the same beginning sound as star?

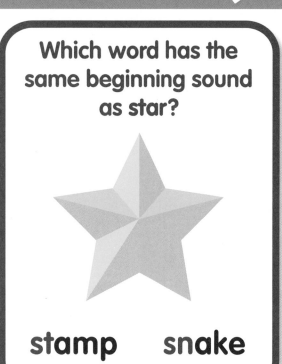

stamp **snake**

Which child is angry?

What do you call a doctor who takes care of animals?

What mark do you put at the end of a question?

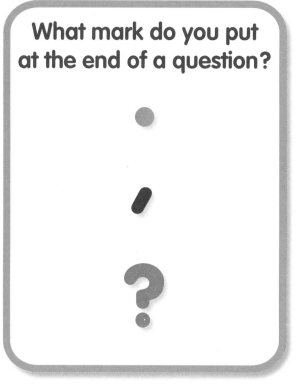

Questions

Subtract the kittens. How many are left?

Look at the picture. Say the word out loud.
Which word rhymes with it?

fun   **hug**   **sun**

bug

I am pretty. You wear me on your finger. I am a _____.

wing   **king**   **ring**

How many words end with an "e"?

money

pie

bone

I am used to wash dishes. I hold water. I am a

_____.

mink

sink

rink

Which number has a 6 in the tens place?

64

46

What language do people from Mexico speak?

French

Spanish

German

Question

Follow the words with the short U sound
to get the bus to the museum.

Which word has the soft C sound you hear in city?

carrot

celery

cat

Which car came in sixth?

Which group has more?

Which word has the same beginning sound as spy?

stomach

sponge

shadow

There were eight students on the bus.
Then five got off.
How many are left?

8
- 5
―――――

Look at the picture.
Say the word out loud.
Which word rhymes
with it?

cow

now   not

Which group has fewer?

Questions

For solutions, turn to page 106.

Which word has the same end sound as lunch?

touch   **tough**

How do you say "good-bye" in Spanish?

hola

adiós

gracias

Eric saw three dogs at the park. He saw six more dogs on the way home. How many dogs in all?

Change the first letter in "rake" to get a baked treat. What letter did you use?

_ake

Which word has the same beginning sound as smile?

small   **short**

What do these letters spell backward?

T - O - P

You use me to tell time. I am a _____.

clock   **lock**

How many are in a full set of adult teeth?

How do you say "hello" in Spanish?

gracias

adiós

hola

Add the penguins.

5 + 3 = ___

Find your way through the maze by following all of the pictures that have a long A like the word "ape."

Which thing in this picture is the wrong color?

I fly in the sky. I take people near and far. I am a _____.

jet

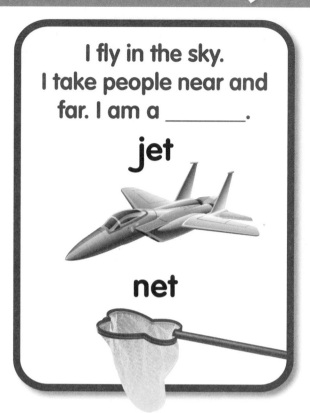

net

The Pacific and Atlantic are kinds of what?

oceans

lakes

rivers

What does the girl need to put on before she can ride her bike?

What do you get when you mix **black** and white?

There are nine watermelon slices. You eat one.
How many are left?

—   =

_____

Do these pictures have a
short or long I sound?

ice

bicycle

mice

Which word ends with
the same sound as laugh?

graph

grass

What numbers are missing?

66 _____ 68 69

_____ _____

Do these pictures have a short or long A sound?

bat

apple

antelope

The judge gave out five red ribbons and eight blue ribbons. How many did he give away in all?

GOOD JOB!

Honorable Mention

Which is the first-place ribbon?

Which pig is the wrong color?

What is the name for the type of animal that keeps its babies in a pouch?

How many letters are in the alphabet?

A B C D E F

G H I J K L

M N O P Q

R S T U V

W X Y Z

Which word has the same beginning sound as cat?

can **cereal**

What animal does bacon come from?

Which things pictured have a short E sound like you hear in sled?

ten

10

apple

turtle

nest

pencil

red

mouse

Ricky wants to make green paint.
Which two colors should he mix?

Ar, matey! Help the pirate point to
all the pictures that contain the "ar" sound.

Put these words in alphabetical order.

cat

apple

bee

How do you say this number?

79

What numbers are missing?

____ 78 ____

80 81 ____

83 ____ 85

Which word has the same end sound as mask?

dish   desk

Look at the picture. Say the word out loud. Which word rhymes with it?

bag   tall   fill

ball

Which pair is being polite?

Which of these need water to live?

What do these letters spell backward?

T - A - B

Which word has the same beginning sound as snake?

skunk   snail

You must only call 911 in case of a real emergency.

true or **false**

How many letters in the alphabet are always vowels?

A B C D E F
G H I J K L
M N O P Q
R S T U V
W X Y Z

Which word has the same ending sound as whale?

ball　　**male**

What numerals mean the same as these words?

eighty-six

_____ _____

What do these letters spell backward?

G-U-M

What kind of story usually starts with "once upon a time"?

fairy tale
nursery rhyme

Which word has the same beginning sound as chick?

chair   **candle**

Which one is another word for happy?

glad

mad

sad

You catch eighteen fish. Seven of them are too small to keep. How many fish do you have?

18 - 7 = _____

Which word has the same beginning sound as slice?

skip   slug

What kind of animal starts out as a tadpole?

frog

fish

Subtract these birds.

Change the first letter in "mug" to get an insect. What letter did you use?

_ug

Questions

For solutions, turn to page 122.

You buy ten pencils. You find another six at home.
How many do you have?

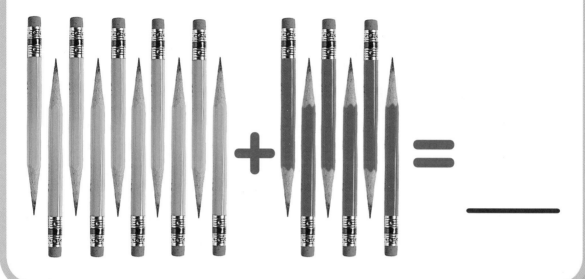

Which picture shows the compound word
these two words make?

gold   fish

Add these numbers.

$$5$$
$$+ 1$$
$$\overline{\hspace{3cm}}$$

Which word has the same ending sound as teeth?

bath   **beach**

Point to where the brain is.

During what month do we celebrate St. Patrick's Day?

March

April

May

You have fifteen shells in your bucket.
Three fall out. How many do you have left?

$$\begin{array}{r} 15 \\ -\ 3 \\ \hline \end{array}$$

Match the weather to the proper clothing.

What kind of animal takes a long sleep during the winter?

horse

bear

cat

Questions

Subtract these numbers.

$$7 - 5$$

Do these pictures have a short or long O sound?

rose

goat

boat

What do you call the area between the words on these books?

There were seven cars in the lot. We saw three drive away. How many are left?

Anna had five books.
Tony gave her five more.
How many books in all?

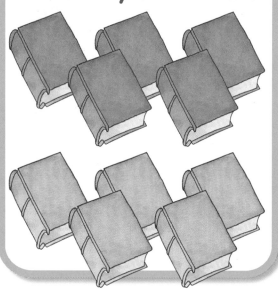

Look at the picture.
Say the word out loud.
Which word rhymes
with it?

house
nose mouse

Subtract these numbers.

18
- 5
———

When you sneeze,
you should cover
your _____.

ears & eyes

nose & mouth

head & shoulders

What kind of animal has a very long neck?

gorilla

or

giraffe

Which one do you use to add and subtract numbers?

camera

calculator

ruler

Fill in the blank to find a shorter way to say this sentence.

I cannot go to the movies today.

I _____ go to the movies today.

You picked fourteen blueberries. Your sister picked six. How many blueberries do you have together?

$14 + 6 = $ _____

Which number has the 1 in the hundreds place?

71   125   15

How do you say "please" in Spanish?

adiós

amigo

por favor

Which number has a 4 in the ones place?

84

48

Solve the equation.

63
+ 4
____

Change the last letter in "coil" to get a kind of money. What letter did you use?

coi_

Which state is farther west: Utah or Iowa?

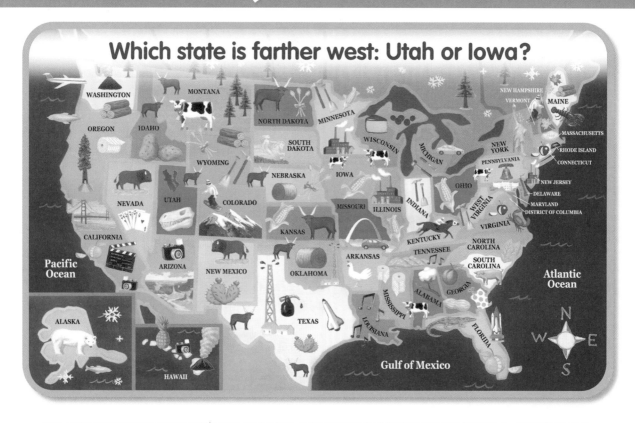

Which foods do NOT belong to the dairy group?

milk

ice cream

cheese

yogurt

egg

apple

What numbers are missing?

92 ___ 94 ___ 96

Which one is the teenager?

There are four red trucks and five blue trucks. How many trucks in all?

Solve the equation.

$$36 - 4$$

What shape is this structure you might find in Egypt?

If you're facing north, what direction is to your left?

Which time is longer?

10 seconds

or

10 hours

Do these words rhyme?

cow

snow

The leader of the United States is called the_____.

king

president

emperor

Solve the equation.

44
− 3
___

Fill in the blank to find a shorter way to say this sentence.

It was not raining.

It _____ raining.

Which person's name has the same middle sound you hear in laundry?

Paul   **Peter**

What do you use to see?

nose

ears

eyes

Which word starts with dog and means a place for a pet to live?

Fido

Solve the equation.

20
+ 7
___

Put these numbers in order from smallest to largest.

83   48   19   32   27

Which picture shows the middle of the story?

Finish the pattern.

Which word has the same middle sound you hear in cloud?

house   school

The Mississippi is a kind of _____.

river

lake

ocean

Solve the equation.

17
+ 2
___

What number would you round 71 to?

70

or

80

Question

Troy and Priscilla's birthday presents start with the same sounds as their names. Which gifts are Priscilla's?

How tall is Andy?

_____ feet & _____ inches

Count by 2's. How many gloves are there?

Questions

What number comes next?

5, 10, 15, 20, _____

Add the numbers in the building.

$$\begin{array}{r} 1 \\ 2 \\ + 3 \\ \hline \end{array}$$

Molly just broke her mom's favorite vase. How do you think she feels?

happy

sad

What season is it if we're dressing up for Halloween?

summer
fall
winter
spring

What's another way to say "he is"?

What mark do you put at the end of a regular sentence?

Which one is taller?

mountain
or
hill

Put these numbers in order from largest to smallest.

63   24   12   81   29

Look at the clues. Put them together. What is the word?

＋   ＝ _____

Count by 10's. What numbers are missing?

10 20 | 40 | 60 70 80 | 100

What's another way to say "they are"?

If you wanted to make the sound of thunder, which instrument would you use?

whistle

guitar

drum

What number would you round 68 to?

60

or

70

Fill in the blank to find a shorter way to say this sentence.

It is not time to go.

It _____ time to go.

Questions

Which numbers come next?

100 90 ___ 70 60

50 ___ 30 20 ___

Point to all the pictures that contain the "or" sound.

Where would you find the Statue of Liberty?

Which word is correct?

Lucy is / be my best friend.

What's a shorter way to say this sentence?

She will not forget her sister's birthday.

She _____ forget.

Subtract the numbers.

77
- 3
_____

Questions

I look similar to a guitar. You play me with a bow.

flute

violin

tuba

Which continent does sushi come from?

What number comes next?

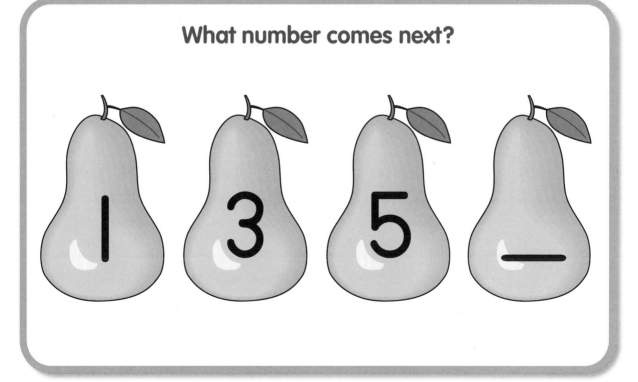

How many continents are there?

Which picture shows the compound word these two words make?

 cow boy

Questions

Point to the words in this sentence where Y sounds like the long I.

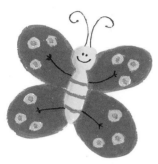

The pretty butterfly flutters by.

Is a chameleon a type of lizard, frog, or fish?

Fill in the missing letter. Use the picture to help you.

rop_

What is the correct way to spell this word?

clown   cloun

What's another way to say "I am"?

Which word has the same sound you hear in boy?

truck toy

Which word in this sentence is the verb?

He reads books.

Where do people get cavities?

Questions

What number comes next?

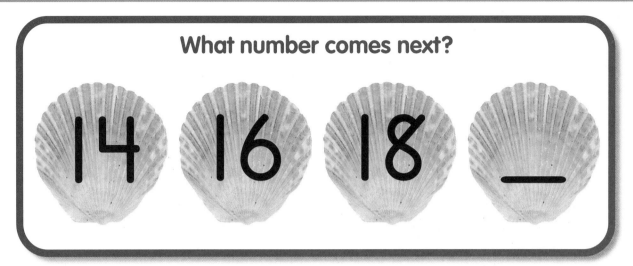

Which object has two sides that look the same?

Put these words in alphabetical order.

ball

bull

bell

What is the opposite of tall?

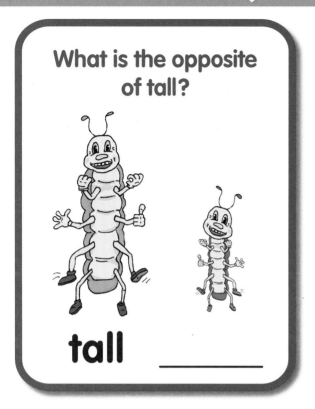

tall _____

What kind of doctor is the boy visiting?

Add the numbers in the building.

$$\begin{array}{r} 2 \\ 3 \\ + 4 \\ \hline \end{array}$$

Which word has the same middle sound as hook?

goose

wood

What do we celebrate on January 1st?

Halloween

Christmas

New Year's Day

Put these words in alphabetical order.

camel

cactus

caboose

Which number is the greatest?

What do the letters on the compass stand for?

What's a shorter way to say this sentence?

He did not hear the boy yelling.

He _____ hear.

Add the numbers.

23

+ 6

Which word means
the opposite of big?

small   long

Say this word.
How many syllables
do you hear?

cupcake

Count the dimes by 10's.
How much are all of
these worth?

Which word means the opposite of cold?

wet hot

Which is another way to say sad?

red
___
blue

Count by 5's. What numbers are missing?

10   15 ___   25   30

35 ___   45   50 ___

Questions

Which objects have the "er" sound?

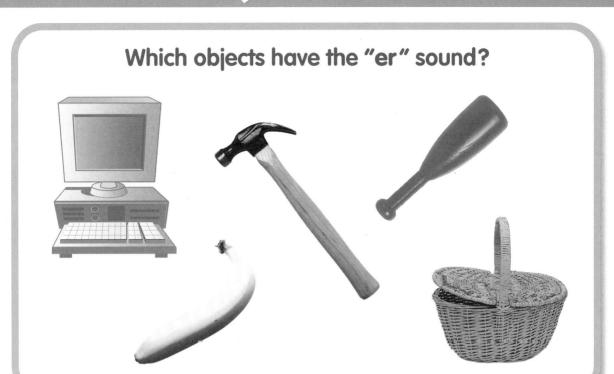

What do you call a group of players?

Question

For solution, turn to page 156.

Point to the lungs.

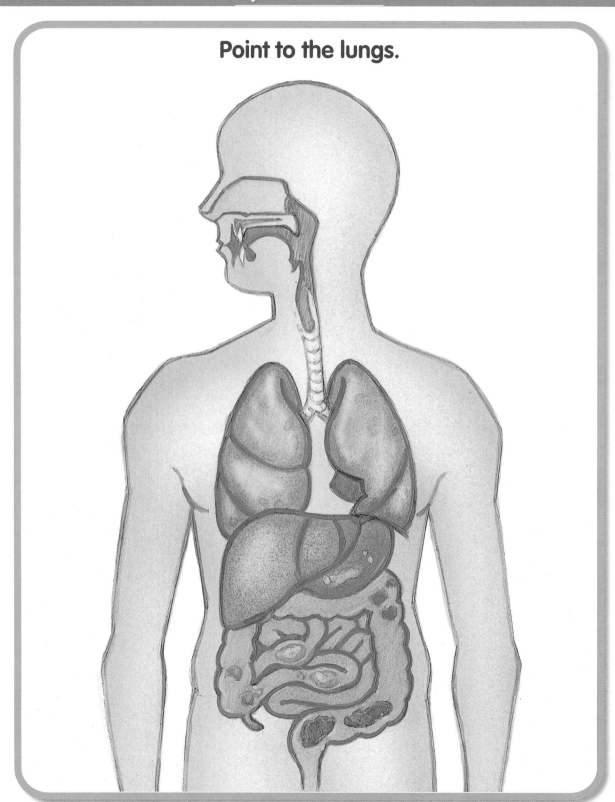

Questions

What happened first?

  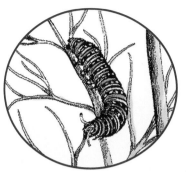

Which number is less?

Which word in this sentence is the verb?

She rides a scooter.

Questions

For solutions, turn to page 158.

Subtract these numbers.

49
- 8
___

What is the correct way to spell the word?

taun town

Which food group do these belong to?

Which is the seventh month?

January

June

July

Subtract these numbers.

$$
\begin{array}{r}
55 \\
-4 \\
\hline
\end{array}
$$

Which word in this sentence is the noun?

The man is strong.

A laptop is a kind of ...

computer
—————
television

Say this word. How many syllables do you hear?

grandmother

Which word in this sentence is the noun?

The girl paints.

What's another word for the season known as autumn?

What color should the last crayon be?

What letter would you add to say more than one boat?

boat_

Questions

Where would you find Big Ben?

Paris
London
Rome

What will happen to this ice cube if you leave it out in the sun?

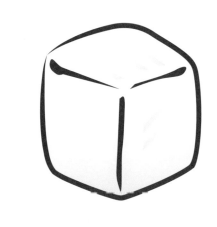

We are more than one man. We are a group of ...

Which glass is least full?

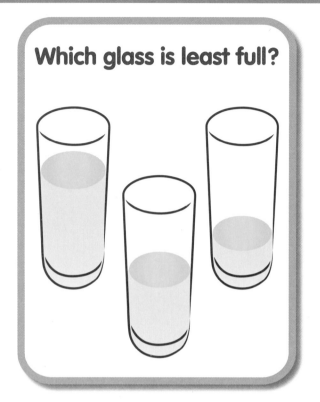

What letter would you add to say more than one cow?

COW_

Which person is the youngest?

Questions

How much is this worth?

Lou wants half of the pizza. How many pieces would he eat?

There were five cows grazing by the creek. Seven horses joined them. How many total animals are there?

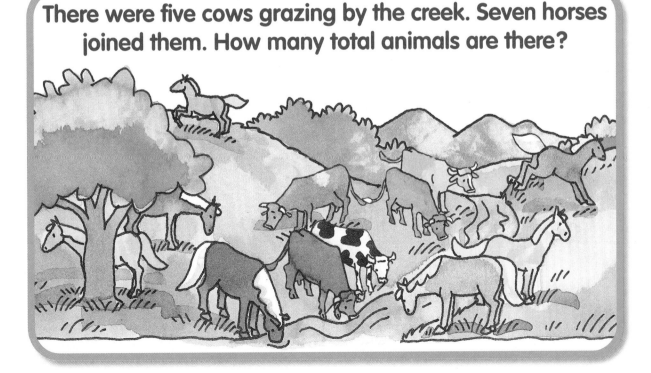

Which two letters can you add to this verb in order to make it past tense?

Yesterday we kick___ the soccer ball.

By the end of the story, what did the ugly duckling become?

Which walrus is smaller?

Which is the correct way to say more than one mouse?

mice

mouses

Questions

Which one is faster?

What do we call the force that keeps us from floating up into the air?

gravity   mass   heat

What's the name for something your body gets from healthy foods?

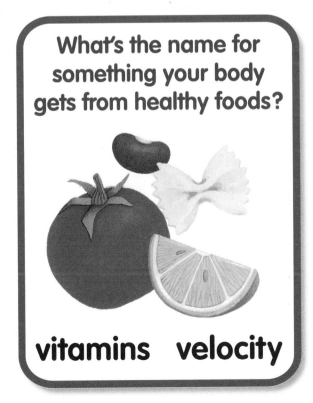

vitamins   velocity

Where can you look up Web sites and read e-mail?

What kind of building keeps people's money safe?

What time is it?

Do you measure height by inches or by pounds?

Which thermometer shows the higher temperature? How many degrees does it show?

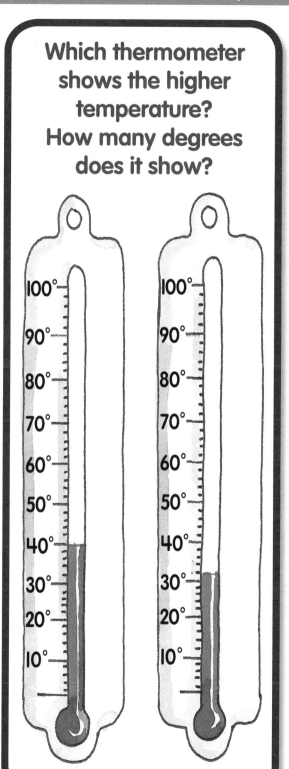

Which one rhymes with socks?

Which word would you use in this sentence?

My mom made
I / me dinner.

Does a submarine usually ride above or under the water?

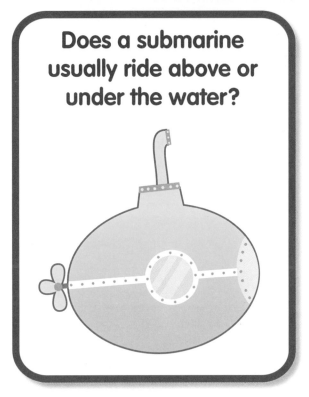

How many minutes are there in one hour?

What does your heart pump through your body?

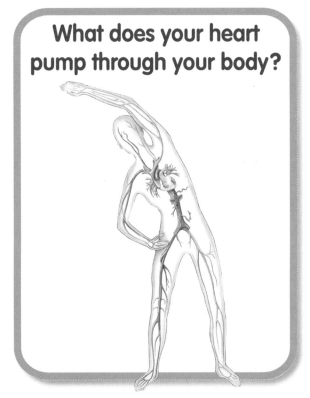

Questions

Which body parts do you mainly use to carry things?

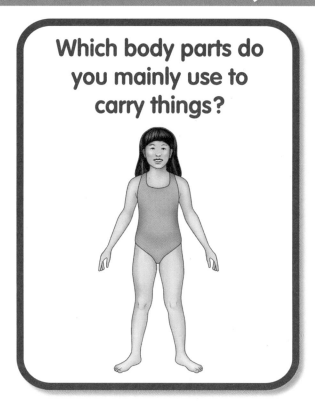

Which stack would be heavier to carry?

Which is less?

pint

cup

What color is the inside of a kiwi?

The Revolutionary War was fought between the United States and ...

England

France

Spain

Which equation is equal to the one in the blue box?

$5+3$

$5+2$

$3+5$

$3+6$

Which item can you buy with this money?

$5

$4

Questions

What do you call this artist's tool?

True or false: The Sun is a star.

How many days are in one year?

Which takes more time?

Can this animal fly?

Finish this phrase.

Reduce, reuse, _____.

What's a shorter way to say "the ball that belongs to Martha"?

Martha__ ball

Which hand on this clock shows minutes?

Question

What feature do these instruments all have in common?

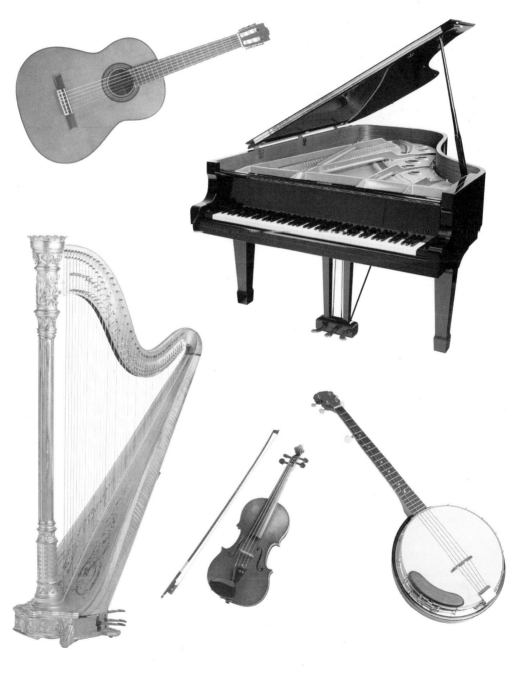

If there are puddles on the ground, what kind of weather did we just have?

What letters would you add to say more than one fox?

fox___

Fill in the missing number for this equation.

$$7 - \underline{} = 4$$

Which words in the sentence should always get capital letters?

eric and i played on sunday.

How many objects have straight sides?

What letter do you need to finish all the words in this picture?

Dadd__

Momm__

kitt__

bab__

pupp__

What letter would you add to say more than one car?

car__

Which words in this sentence should always get capital letters?

james has a birthday in july.

Dan ate a quarter of the pie. How many pieces did he eat?

How much is this worth?

Questions

Which is the correct way to spell more than one penny?

pennys
***
pennies

Fill in the missing number for this equation.

$$6$$
$$+ \underline{\qquad}$$
$$\overline{\ 10}$$

Which building is the second tallest?

What time is it?

Which clock shows the same time as the one in the yellow box?

True or false: The tongue is a kind of muscle.

Who is sleeping in Baby Bear's bed?

Which word is correct?

We goed / went **for a swim.**

True or false: The Moon is a planet.

How many weeks are there in a year?

Which is the connecting word in this sentence?

I have a pen and a pencil.

What time is it?

An adjective is a word that describes a noun. Which word is the adjective?

tall tower

Which equation is equal to the one in the orange box?

4+1

1+1

3+1

2+1

1+4

Questions

How many eggs are in a dozen?

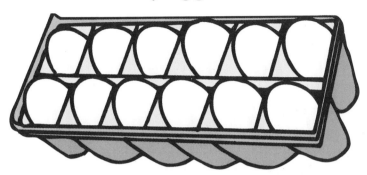

Who are these two fairy-tale children?

Is this a sentence?

The bear stands.

Which two letters can you add to this verb in order to make it past tense?

The kids jump__ over the puddles.

What number is equal to three groups of three?

Finish the poem.

Twinkle, twinkle, little _____,
How I wonder what you are.

How many of these foods belong to the grains group?

Which animal is extinct?

Is this a sentence?

The boy bike.

Do you think this mask would be used in a sad or a funny play?

In the story, who scared Miss Muffet away?

An adverb is a word that describes a verb or adjective. Which word is the adverb?

He runs quickly.

Look at the picture. What story is this?

How likely is it to pull a red crayon from this box? Likely, unlikely, or impossible?

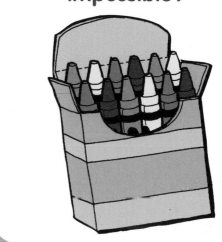

If four friends find $1 and share it equally, how much money would each get?

What time is it?

Question

For solution, turn to page 186.

How many planets are in the solar system?

Questions

Which two letters can you add to this verb in order to make it past tense?

They play__ music.

How do you say "yes" in French?

non

oui

Who lost her sheep?

Which picture best completes the sentence?

The _____ flies at night.

Which is the correct way to say more than one foot?

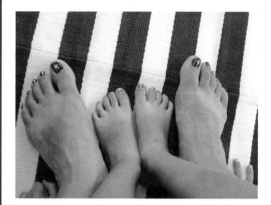

foots   feet

Whose nose grew when he lied?

Which word is correct?

The cat getted / got the ball.

Questions

Which box shows two words that mean the same thing?

bird
wing

late
early

cat
dog

tired
sleepy

circle
square

start
end

yes
no

up
down

Point to the comet.

Which one means "good-bye" in French?

bonjour

au revoir

Which picture best completes the sentence?

I write with a _____.

Which item can you buy with this money?

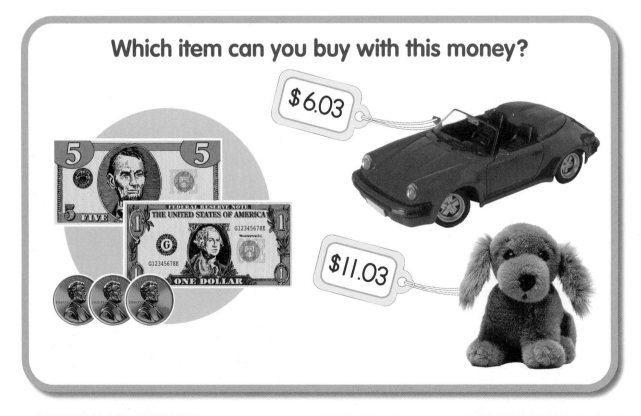

$6.03

$11.03

Which letters would you add to say more than one dish?

dish____

What color is the inside of a pineapple?

Is this a sentence?

Roller coasters are fun.

Who are these nursery-rhyme characters?

Answers for page 4

Which word has the same ending sound as nest?

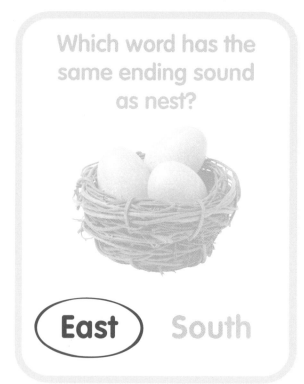

East South

Which two groups have an equal number of fruits?

Which animal starts the same way as goose?

goat

Is the girl doing **gymnastics** or gymnasium?

Fill in the missing note at the end to finish the pattern.

You have five ice pops. Your friend has two.
How many ice pops do you have together?

+ = 7

You have two quarters. Point to what you can buy.

50¢ or 25¢ 95¢

Answers for page 6

Which word has the same beginning sound as star?

stamp snake

Which child is angry?

What do you call a doctor who takes care of animals?

veterinarian

What mark do you put at the end of a question?

?

question mark

Answers for page 7

Subtract the kittens. How many are left?

 = 0

Look at the picture. Say the word out loud. Which word rhymes with it?

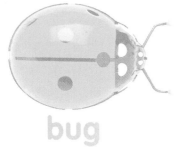

bug

fun (hug) sun

I am pretty. You wear me on your finger. I am a _____.

wing king **ring**

Answers for page 8

How many words end with an "e"?

money

pie

bone

2

I am used to wash dishes. I hold water. I am a

_____.

mink

sink

rink

Which number has a 6 in the tens place?

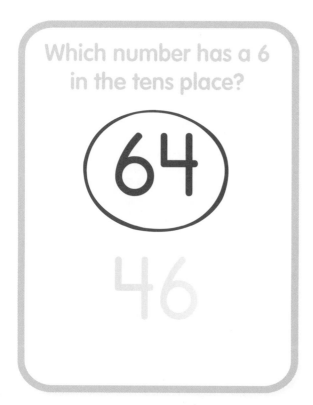

64

46

What language do people from Mexico speak?

French

Spanish

German

Follow the words with the short U sound
to get the bus to the museum.

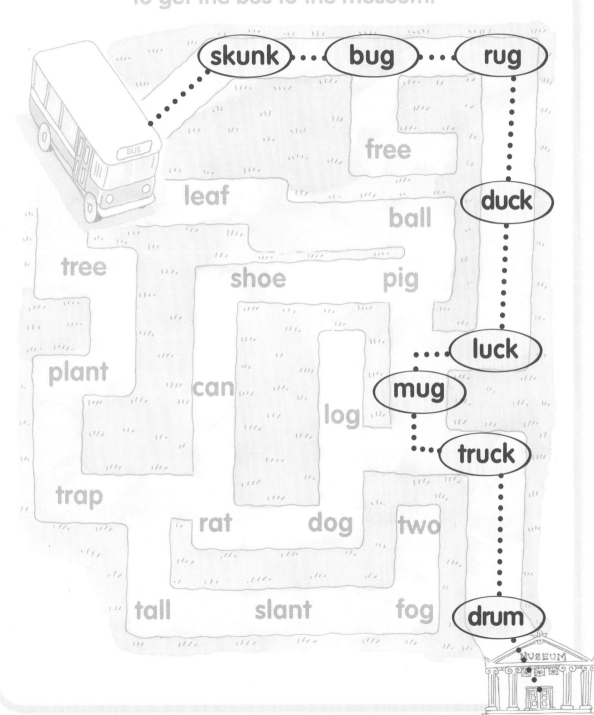

Which word has the soft C sound you hear in city?

carrot

celery

cat

Which car came in sixth?

2

4

3

6

1

5

Which group has more?

15

12

Which word has the same beginning sound as spy?

stomach

sponge

shadow

There were eight students on the bus.
Then five got off.
How many are left?

$$\begin{array}{r} 8 \\ -\ 5 \\ \hline 3 \end{array}$$

Look at the picture.
Say the word out loud.
Which word rhymes
with it?

cow

(now)   not

Which group has fewer?

12

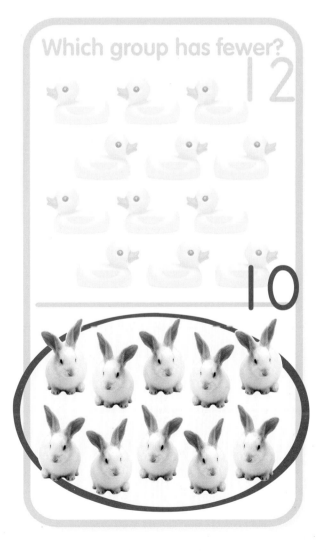

10

Answers for page 12

Which word has the same end sound as lunch?

touch tough

How do you say "good-bye" in Spanish?

hola

adiós

gracias

Eric saw three dogs at the park. He saw six more dogs on the way home. How many dogs in all?

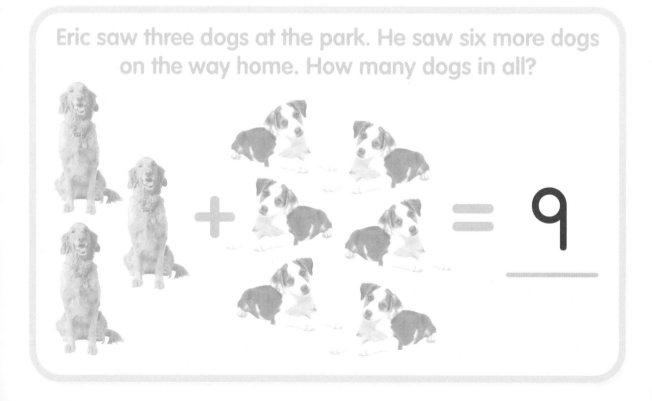

$+$ $=$ 9

Change the first letter in "rake" to get a baked treat. What letter did you use?

<u>c</u>ake

Which word has the same beginning sound as smile?

small short

What do these letters spell backward?

T - O - P

POT

You use me to tell time. I am a _____.

clock lock

Answers for page 14

How many are in a full set of adult teeth?

32

How do you say "hello" in Spanish?

gracias

adiós

hola

Add the penguins.

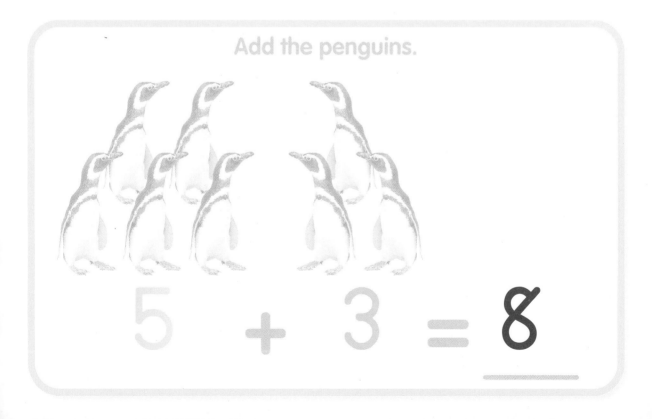

5 + 3 = 8

Answers for page 15

Find your way through the maze by following all of the pictures that have a long A like the word "ape."

START

snake

rake

vase

cake

FINISH

Which thing in this picture is the wrong color?

blue dog

Answers for page 16

I fly in the sky.
I take people near and
far. I am a _____.

jet

net

The Pacific and Atlantic
are kinds of what?

oceans

lakes

rivers

What does the girl need
to put on before she
can ride her bike?

helmet

What do you get when
you mix black and white?

gray

There are nine watermelon slices. You eat one. How many are left?

$- = 8$

Do these pictures have a short or (long I) sound?

ice

bicycle

mice

Which word ends with the same sound as laugh?

(graph)

grass

Answers for page 18

What numbers are missing?

65 66 67 68 69

Do these pictures have a (short) or long A sound?

apple

bat

antelope

The judge gave out five red ribbons and eight blue ribbons. How many did he give away in all?

5 + 8 = 13

GOOD JOB!

Honorable Mention

Which is the first-place ribbon?

Which pig is the wrong color?

purple pig

What is the name for the type of animal that keeps its babies in a pouch?

marsupial

How many letters are in the alphabet?

A B C D E F
G H I J K L
M N O P Q
R S T U V
W X Y Z

26

Answers for page 20

Which word has the same beginning sound as cat?

(can) cereal

What animal does bacon come from?

pig

Which things pictured have a short E sound like you hear in sled?

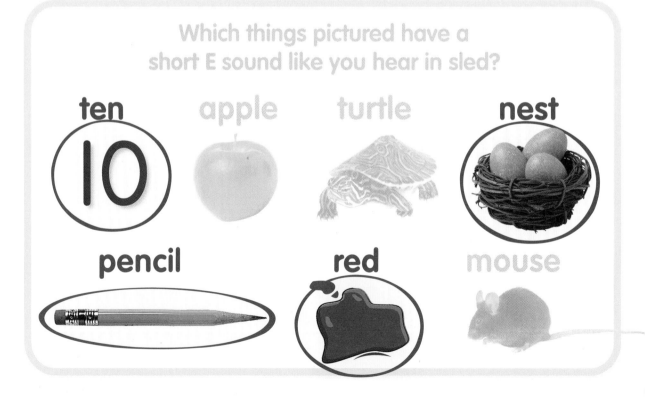

ten   apple   turtle   nest

10

pencil   red   mouse

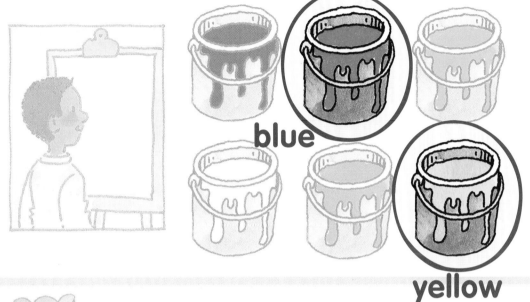

Ricky wants to make green paint.
Which two colors should he mix?

blue

yellow

Ar, matey! Help the pirate point to
all the pictures that contain the "ar" sound.

car

dart

star

Put these words
in alphabetical order.

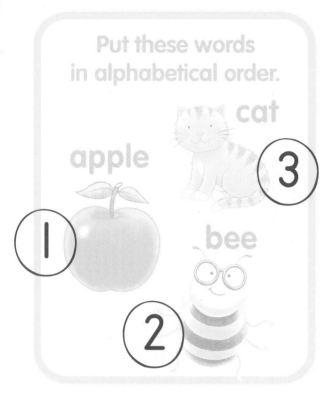

cat

apple

③

①

bee

②

How do you say
this number?

79

seventy-nine

What numbers
are missing?

77 78 **79**

80 81 **82**

83 **84** 85

Which word has the same
end sound as mask?

dish (**desk**)

Look at the picture. Say the word out loud.
Which word rhymes with it?

bag (tall) fill

ball

Which pair
is being polite?

Which of these
need water to live?

fish

flower

boy

What do these letters spell backward?

T - A - B

BAT

Which word has the same beginning sound as snake?

skunk   (snail)

You must only call 911 in case of a real emergency.

(true) or false

How many letters in the alphabet are always vowels?

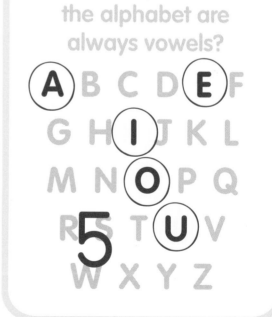

(A) B C D (E) F
G H (I) J K L
M N (O) P Q
R **5** T (U) V
W X Y Z

Which word has the same ending sound as whale?

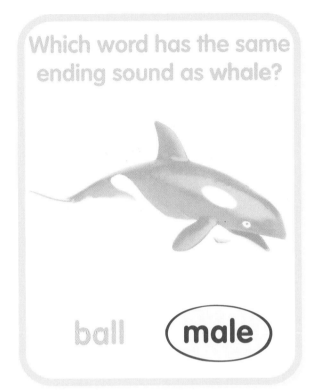

ball **male**

What numerals mean the same as these words?

eighty-six

86

_____ _____

What do these letters spell backward?

G - U - M

MUG

What kind of story usually starts with "once upon a time"?

fairy tale

nursery rhyme

Which word has the same beginning sound as chick?

(chair) candle

Which one is another word for happy?

(glad)

mad

sad

You catch eighteen fish. Seven of them are too small to keep. How many fish do you have?

18 - 7 = 11

Which word has the same beginning sound as slice?

skip **slug**

What kind of animal starts out as a tadpole?

frog

fish

Subtract these birds.

2

Change the first letter in "mug" to get an insect. What letter did you use?

bug

Answers for page 28

You buy ten pencils. You find another six at home.
How many do you have?

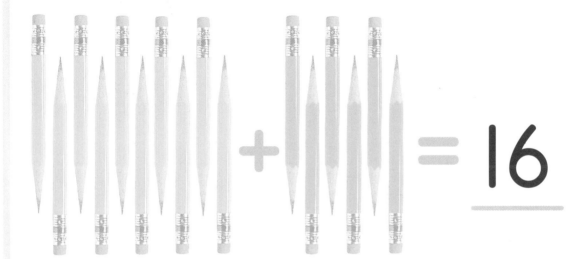

Which picture shows the compound word
these two words make?

gold   fish

newspaper   **goldfish**   ladybug

Add these numbers.

$$5$$
$$+1$$
$$\overline{6}$$

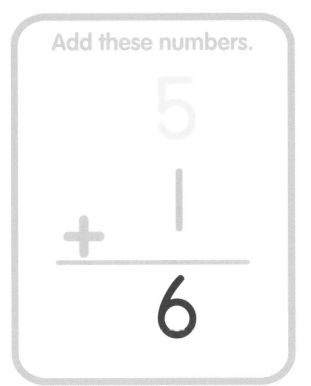

Which word has the same ending sound as teeth?

bath beach

Point to where the brain is.

head

During what month do we celebrate St. Patrick's Day?

March

April

May

Answers for page 30

You have fifteen shells in your bucket.
Three fall out. How many do you have left?

$$15 - 3 = 12$$

Match the weather to
the proper clothing.

What kind of animal
takes a long sleep during
the winter?

horse

bear

cat

Subtract these numbers.

$$
\begin{array}{r}
7 \\
-\ 5 \\
\hline
2
\end{array}
$$

Do these pictures have a short or **long O** sound?

rose

goat

boat

What do you call the area between the words on these books?

spaces

There were seven cars in the lot. We saw three drive away. How many are left?

4

Anna had five books.
Tony gave her five more.
How many books in all?

10

Look at the picture.
Say the word out loud.
Which word rhymes
with it?

house
nose (mouse)

Subtract these numbers.

18
- 5

13

When you sneeze,
you should cover
your _____.

ears & eyes

(nose & mouth)

head & shoulders

What kind of animal has a very long neck?

gorilla

or

giraffe

Which one do you use to add and subtract numbers?

camera

calculator

ruler

Answers for page 34

Fill in the blank to find a shorter way to say this sentence.

I cannot go to the movies today.

I **can't** go to the movies today.

You picked fourteen blueberries. Your sister picked six. How many blueberries do you have together?

$14 + 6 = 20$

Which number has the 1 in the hundreds place?

71   (125)   15

How do you say "please" in Spanish?

adiós

amigo

por favor

Which number has a 4 in the ones place?

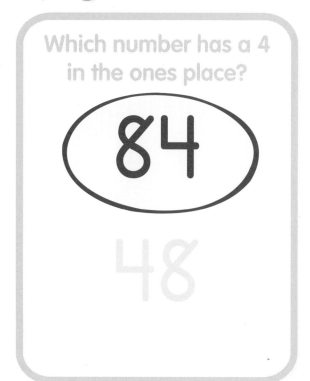

84

48

Solve the equation.

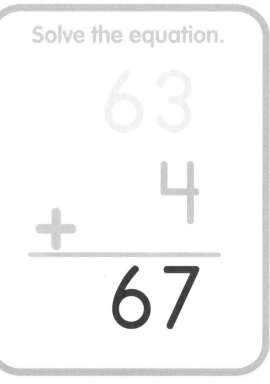

$$63 + 4 = 67$$

Change the last letter in "coil" to get a kind of money.
What letter did you use?

coin

130

Answers for page 36

Which state is farther west, Utah or Iowa?

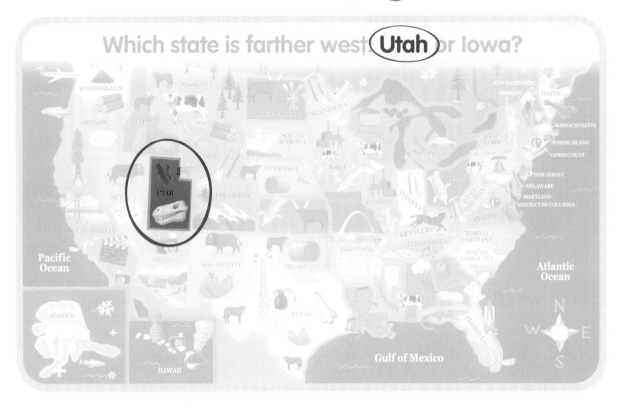

Which foods do NOT belong to the dairy group?

milk

ice cream

cheese

yogurt

egg

apple

What numbers are missing?

92 **93** 94 **95** 96

Which one is the teenager?

There are four red trucks and five blue trucks. How many trucks in all?

9

Solve the equation.

$$\begin{array}{r} 36 \\ 4 \\ \hline 32 \end{array}$$

What shape is this structure you might find in Egypt?

pyramid

If you're facing north, what direction is to your left?

west

Which time is longer?

10 seconds

or

10 hours

Do these words rhyme?

cow

no

snow

The leader of the
United States is called
the _____.

king

president

emperor

Solve the equation.

44

3

−

41

Fill in the blank to find a
shorter way to say
this sentence.

It was not raining.

It _____ **wasn't** _____ raining.

Answers for page 40

Which person's name has the same middle sound you hear in laundry?

Paul   Peter

What do you use to see?

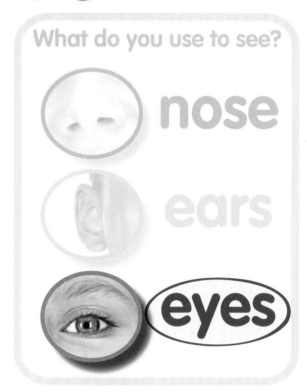

nose

ears

eyes

Which word starts with dog and means a place for a pet to live?

Fido

doghouse

Solve the equation.

$$\begin{array}{r} 20 \\ 7 \\ + \\ \hline 27 \end{array}$$

Answers for page 41

Put these numbers in order from smallest to largest.

83   48   19   32   27

⑤   ④   ①   ③   ②

Which picture shows the middle of the story?

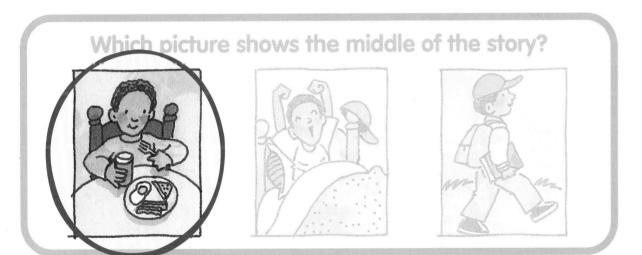

Finish the pattern.

Answers for page 42

Which word has the same middle sound you hear in cloud?

(house) school

The Mississippi is a kind of _____.

(river)

lake

ocean

Solve the equation.

$$\begin{array}{r} 17 \\ +\ 2 \\ \hline 19 \end{array}$$

What number would you round 71 to?

(70)

or

80

Troy and Priscilla's birthday presents start with the same sounds as their names. Which gifts are Priscilla's?

princess

prince

pretzel

Answers for page 44

How tall is Andy?

4 feet & **9** inches

Count by 2's.
How many gloves
are there?

2

4

6

8

10

12

12

What number comes next?

5, 10, 15, 20, __25__

Add the numbers in the building.

```
  1
  2
+ 3
-----
  6
```

Molly just broke her mom's favorite vase. How do you think she feels?

happy

sad

Answers for page 46

What season is it if we're dressing up for Halloween?

summer

fall

winter

spring

What's another way to say "he is"?

he's

What mark do you put at the end of a regular sentence?

period

Which one is taller?

mountain

or

hill

Answers for page 47

Put these numbers in order from largest to smallest.

63 — 2
24 — 4
12 — 5
81 — 1
29 — 3

Look at the clues. Put them together. What is the word?

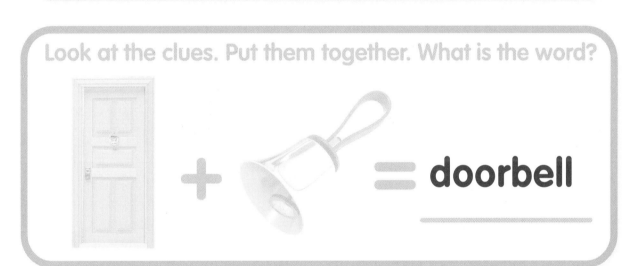

+ = **doorbell**

Count by 10's. What numbers are missing?

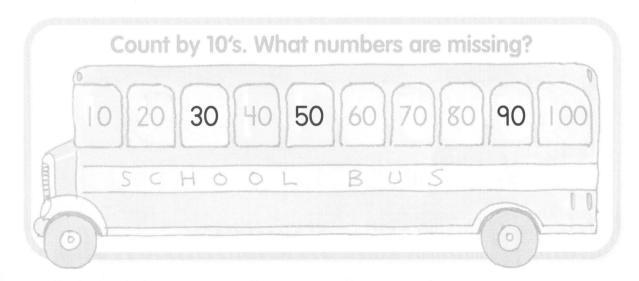

10 20 **30** 40 **50** 60 70 80 **90** 100

SCHOOL BUS

Answers for page 48

What's another way to say "they are"?

they're

If you wanted to make the sound of thunder, which instrument would you use?

whistle

guitar

drum

What number would you round 68 to?

60

or

70

Fill in the blank to find a shorter way to say this sentence.

It is not time to go.

It **isn't** time to go.

Which numbers come next?

100 90 <u>80</u> 70 60

50 <u>40</u> 30 20 <u>10</u>

Point to all the pictures that contain the "or" sound.

orange

horn

corn

Answers for page 50

Where would you find the Statue of Liberty?

New York

Which word is correct?

Lucy (is) be my best friend.

What's a shorter way to say this sentence?

She will not forget her sister's birthday.

She **won't** forget.

Subtract the numbers.

$$\begin{array}{r} 77 \\ -3 \\ \hline 74 \end{array}$$

I look similar to a guitar. You play me with a bow.

flute
violin
tuba

Which continent does sushi come from?

Asia

What number comes next?

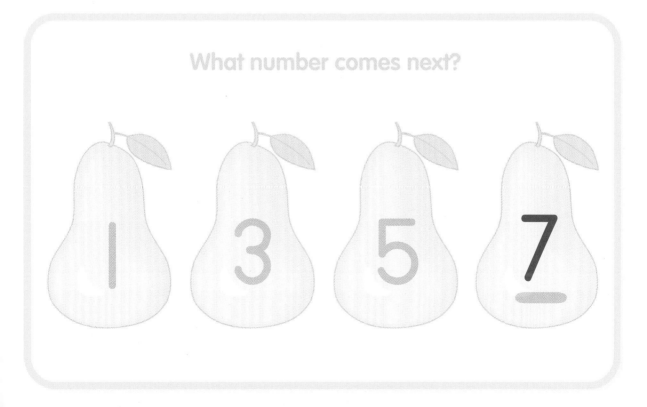

1   3   5   7

Answers for page 52

How many continents are there?

7

Europe

North America

Asia

Africa

South America

Australia

Antarctica

Which picture shows the compound word these two words make?

cow

boy

cowboy

farmer

cowgirl

Point to the words in this sentence where Y sounds like the long I.

The pretty **butterfly** flutters **by**

Is a chameleon a type of **lizard**, frog, or fish?

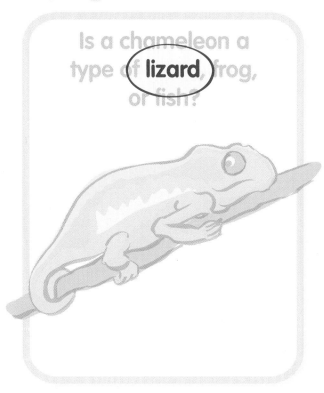

Fill in the missing letter. Use the picture to help you.

rop**e**

What is the correct way to spell this word?

clown cloun

Answers for page 54

What's another way to say "I am"?

I'm

Which word has the same sound you hear in boy?

truck **toy**

Which word in this sentence is the verb?

He **reads** books.

Where do people get cavities?

teeth

What number comes next?

14 16 18 **20**

Which object has two sides that look the same?

jack-o'-lantern

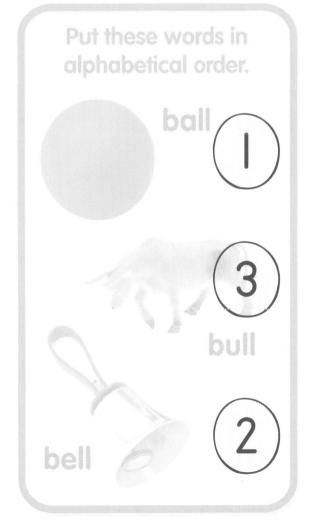

Put these words in alphabetical order.

ball ①

bull ③

bell ②

Answers for page 56

What is the opposite of tall?

tall **short**

What kind of doctor is the boy visiting?

dentist

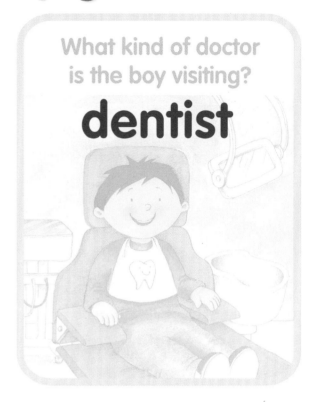

Add the numbers in the building.

2
3
+ 4

9

Which word has the same middle sound as hook?

goose

wood

What do we celebrate on January 1st?

Halloween

Christmas

New Year's Day

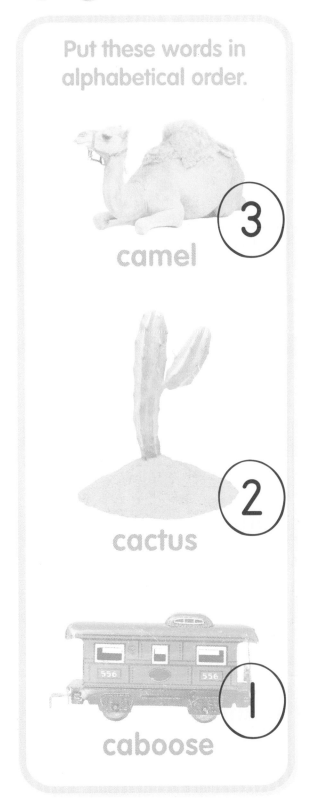

Put these words in alphabetical order.

camel ③

cactus ②

caboose ①

Answers for page 58

Which number is the greatest?

12

90

78

What do the letters on the compass stand for?

North

West   **East**

South

What's a shorter way to say this sentence?

He did not hear the boy yelling.

He **didn't** hear.

Add the numbers.

23
6

$+$
___
29

Which word means
the opposite of big?

(small) long

Say this word.
How many syllables
do you hear?

cup - cake

2

Count the dimes by 10's.
How much are all of
these worth?

10 20 30

90¢

40 50 60

70 80 90

Answers for page 60

Which word means the opposite of cold?

wet **(hot)**

Which is another way to say sad?

red **(blue)**

Count by 5's. What numbers are missing?

10   15   **20**   25   30

35   **40**   45   50   **55**

Which objects have the "er" sound?

hammer

computer

What do you call a group of players?

team

Answer for page 62

Point to the lungs.

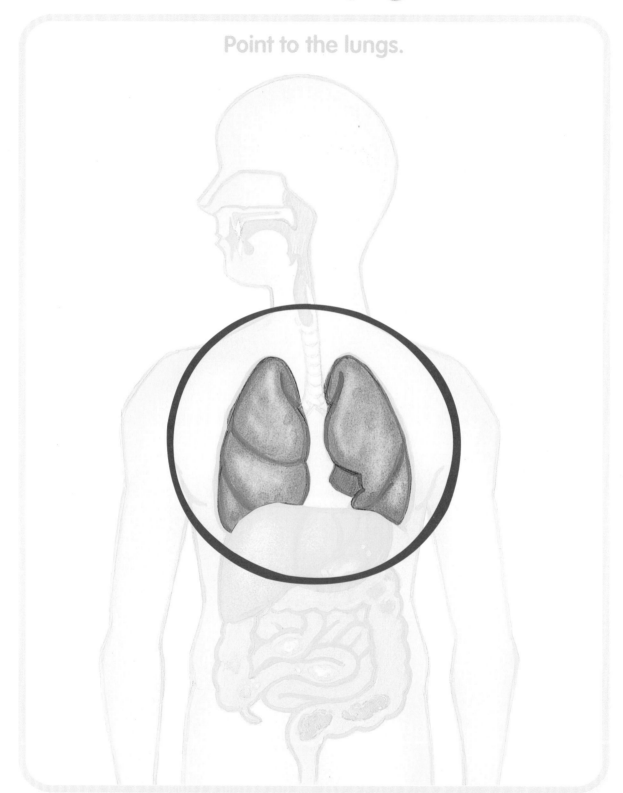

What happened first?

Which number is less?

23

32

Which word in this sentence is the verb?

She rides a scooter.

Answers for page 64

Subtract these numbers.

49
8
-
___
41

What is the correct way to spell the word?

taur **town**

Which food group do these belong to?

meat

Which is the seventh month?

January

June

July

Subtract these numbers.

55
- 4
———
51

Which word in this sentence is the noun?

The **man** is strong.

A laptop is a kind of ...

computer

television

Say this word. How many syllables do you hear?

grand - moth - er

3

Answers for page 66

Which word in this sentence is the noun?

The **girl** paints.

What's another word for the season known as autumn?

fall

What color should the last crayon be?

yellow

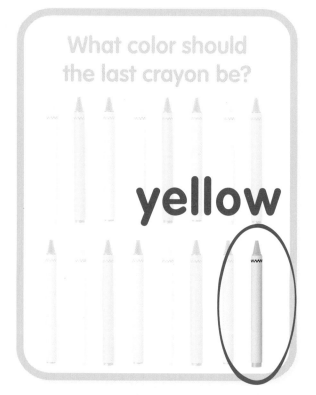

What letter would you add to say more than one boat?

boat<u>s</u>

Where would you find Big Ben?

Paris

London

Rome

What will happen to this ice cube if you leave it out in the sun?

It will melt.

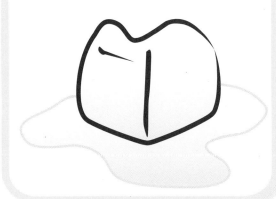

We are more than one man. We are a group of...

men

Answers for page 68

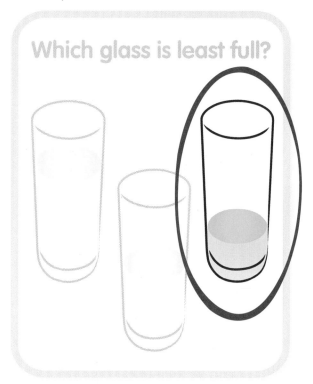

Which glass is least full?

What letter would you add to say more than one cow?

cow**s**

Which person is the youngest?

Answers for page 69

How much is
this worth?

$5.10

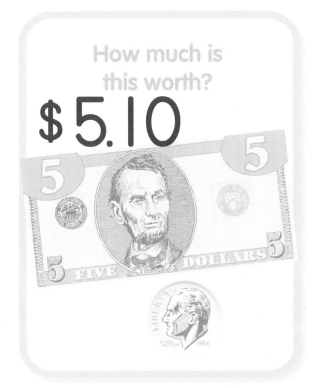

Lou wants half of the
pizza. How many pieces
would he eat?

2

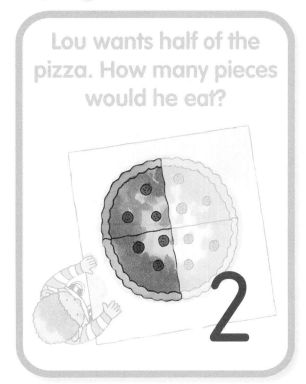

There were five cows grazing by the creek. Seven horses
joined them. How many total animals are there?

12

Which two letters can you add to this verb in order to make it past tense?

Yesterday we kick**ed** the soccer ball.

By the end of the story, what did the ugly duckling become?

swan

Which walrus is smaller?

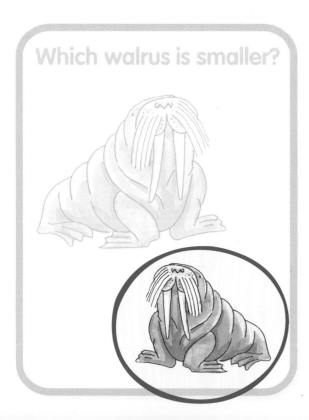

Which is the correct way to say more than one mouse?

mice

mouses

Which one is faster?

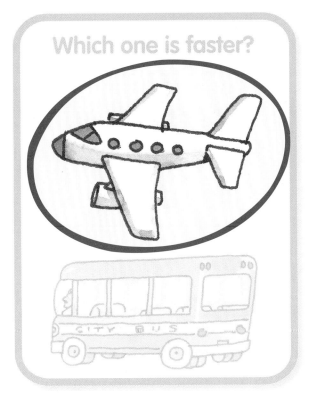

What do we call the force that keeps us from floating up into the air?

gravity mass heat

What's the name for something your body gets from healthy foods?

vitamins velocity

Where can you look up Web sites and read e-mail?

the Internet

Answers for page 72

What kind of building keeps people's money safe?

bank

What time is it?

2:30

Do you measure height by **inches** or by pounds?

Which thermometer shows the higher temperature?
How many degrees does it show?

40°

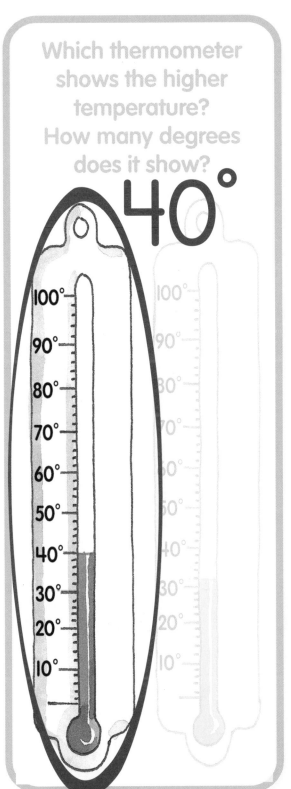

Which one rhymes with socks?

box

Answers for page 74

Which word would you use in this sentence?

My mom made me dinner.

Does a submarine usually ride above or **under** the water?

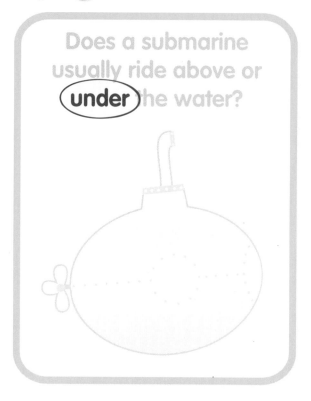

How many minutes are there in one hour?

What does your heart pump through your body?

blood

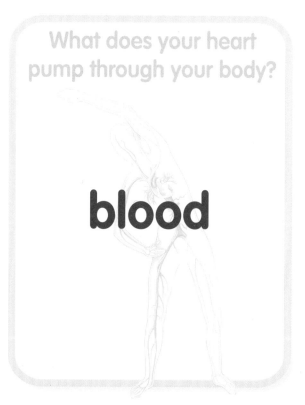

Answers for page 75

Which body parts do you mainly use to carry things?

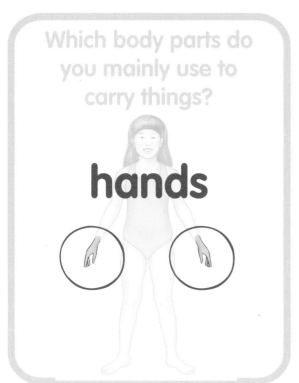

hands

Which stack would be heavier to carry?

Which is less?

pint

cup

What color is the inside of a kiwi?

green

Answers for page 76

The Revolutionary War was fought between the United States and...

England   France   Spain

Which equation is equal to the one in the blue box?

$5+3$

$5+2$

$3+5$

$3+6$

Which item can you buy with this money?

$5

$4

What do you call this artist's tool?

palette

True or false: The Sun is a star.

true

How many days are in one year?

365

Which takes more time?

Can this animal fly?

no

Finish this phrase.

Reduce, reuse, **recycle**.

What's a shorter way to say "the ball that belongs to Martha"?

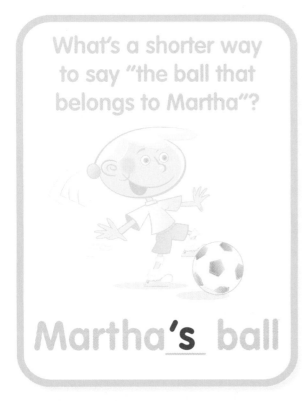

Martha**'s** ball

Which hand on this clock shows minutes?

What feature do these instruments all have in common?

They are all string instruments.

Answers for page 80

If there are puddles on the ground, what kind of weather did we just have?

rain

What letters would you add to say more than one fox?

fox<u>es</u>

Fill in the missing number for this equation.

$$\begin{array}{r} 7 \\ -\ 3 \\ \hline 4 \end{array}$$

Which words in the sentence should always get capital letters?

Eric and **I** played on **Sunday**.

How many objects have straight sides?

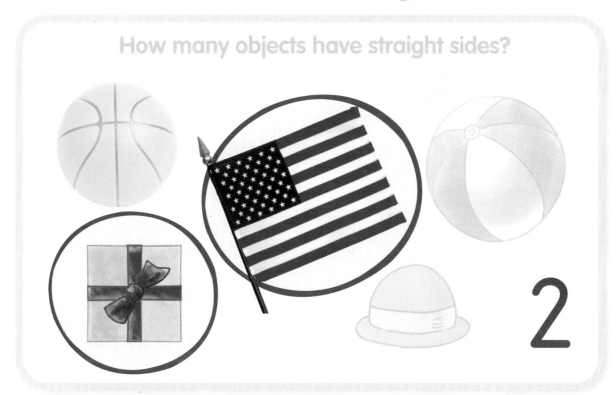

2

What letter do you need to finish
all the words in this picture?

Daddy

Mommy

baby

kitty

puppy

y

Answers for page 82

What letter would you add to say more than one car?

car<u>s</u>

Which words in this sentence should always get capital letters?

James has a **birthday** in **July**.

Dan ate a quarter of the pie. How many pieces did he eat?

1

How much is this worth?

$1.04

Which is the correct way to spell more than one penny?

pennys

(**pennies**)

Fill in the missing number for this equation.

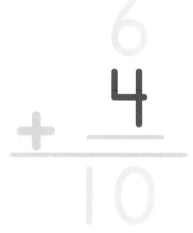

$$\begin{array}{r} 6 \\ + 4 \\ \hline 10 \end{array}$$

Which building is the second tallest?

What time is it?

10:30

Which clock shows the same time as the one in the yellow box?

True or false: The tongue is a kind of muscle.

true

Who is sleeping in Baby Bear's bed?

Goldilocks

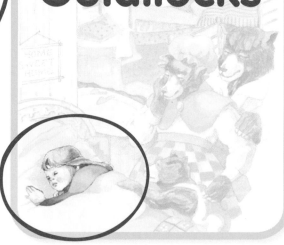

Which word is correct?

We goed **went** for a drive.

True or false:
The Moon is a planet.

false

How many weeks are there in a year?

52

Which is the connecting word in this sentence?

I have a pen **and** a pencil.

What time is it?

7:30

An adjective is a word that describes a noun. Which word is the adjective?

tall tower

Which equation is equal to the one in the orange box?

4+1

1+1   3+1

2+1   **1+4**

How many eggs are in a dozen?

12

Who are these two fairy-tale children?

Hansel and Gretel

Is this a sentence?

yes

The bear stands.

Answers for page 88

Which two letters can you add to this verb
in order to make it past tense?

The kids jump **ed** over the puddles.

What number is equal to three groups of three?

9

Answers for page 89

Finish the poem.

Twinkle, twinkle, little **star**,
How I wonder what you are.

How many of these foods belong to the grains group?

bread

cereal

2

Which animal is extinct?

dinosaur

Is this a sentence?

no

The boy bike.

Do you think this mask would be used in a sad or a funny play?

funny

In the story, who scared Miss Muffet away?

spider

An adverb is a word that describes a verb or adjective. Which word is the adverb?

He runs **quickly**

Look at the picture.
What story is this?

Little Red Riding Hood

How likely is it to pull
a red crayon from this
box? Likely, unlikely, or

impossible?

If four friends find $1 and
share it equally, how much
money would each get?

25¢

What time is it?

3:30

Answer for page 92

How many planets are in the solar system?

Saturn

Uranus

Neptune

Jupiter

8

Mars

Earth

Venus

Mercury

Which two letters can you add to this verb in order to make it past tense?

They play**ed** music.

How do you say "yes" in French?

non

oui

Who lost her sheep?

Little Bo Peep

Which picture best completes the sentence?

The **bat** flies at night.

Which is the correct way to say more than one foot?

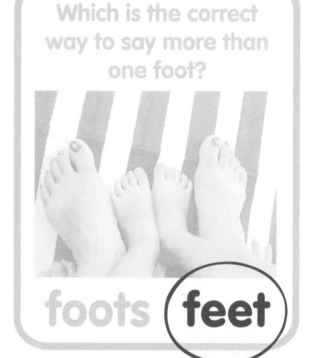

foots **feet**

Whose nose grew when he lied?

Pinocchio

Which word is correct?

The cat getted/**got** the ball.

Which box shows two words that mean the same thing?

bird
wing

late
early

cat
dog

tired
sleepy

circle
square

start
end

yes
no

up
down

Point to the comet.

Answers for page 96

Which one means "good-bye" in French?

bonjour

au revoir

Which picture best completes the sentence?

I write with a **pen**.

Which item can you buy with this money?

$6.03

$11.03

Which letters would you add to say more than one dish?

dish**es**

What color is the inside of a pineapple?

yellow

Is this a sentence?

Roller coasters are fun.

yes

Who are these nursery-rhyme characters?

Three Blind Mice

CONGRATULATIONS!

YOU DID IT!